BETWEEN THE HOURS

poems by

Barbara Siegel Carlson

Finishing Line Press
Georgetown, Kentucky

BETWEEN THE HOURS

Copyright © 2022 by Barbara Siegel Carlson
ISBN 978-1-64662-878-0 First Edition
All rights reserved under International and Pan-American Copyright Conventions. No part of this book may be reproduced in any manner whatsoever without written permission from the publisher, except in the case of brief quotations embodied in critical articles and reviews.

ACKNOWLEDGMENTS

Special thanks to Ana Jelnikar for believing in this body of work and encouraging me to send it out. Thanks also to Mary Kane, Scott Withiam, Miriam O'Neal, Dzvinia Orlowsky and Stephan Delbos. And to Leah, Christen and the others at Finishing Line Press who helped make this chapbook a reality.

Publisher: Leah Huete de Maines
Editor: Christen Kincaid
Cover Art: Barbara Siegel Carlson
Author Photo: Lily Stone
Cover Design: Elizabeth Maines McCleavy

Order online: www.finishinglinepress.com
also available on amazon.com

Author inquiries and mail orders:
Finishing Line Press
PO Box 1626
Georgetown, Kentucky 40324
USA

Table of Contents

Cloud 0 1

To the Wind 2

Small Hours 3

The Lost Hour 4

The Light of Late Winter 5

Passenger 6

To the Darkness 7

A Memory 8

To Sleep 9

Windy Night 10

Lost Book 11

Paradoxical 12

Flowers of Snow 13

Birthday 14

Ten Thousand Things 15

After the Words 16

Gazing at Branches 17

Open the Book to Any Page 18

Return 19

Without a Trace 20

Amid Such Breath 21

Part of Me 22

*For Larry
and for Emmett, Lily and Lizzy*

It is the spirit that holds onto our treasure.
—Jack Gilbert

Cloud 0

There were roads known, but they led to a place not on any map and with no inhabitants. Later, waking up I wanted to return to that place, only to find it had disappeared.

To the Wind

Do you ever want to rest in my bones?
And what would you say to them?

Small Hours

In sleep they seem to shrink if not vanish altogether into half-visions and swiftly moving scenes of a story entire in each fragment. A voice, road, part of a room or door half open. If it's a neighborhood, it's both strange and familiar with an ocean at the back door. If it's a house we grew up in, there are rooms we never saw in a wing we never entered. If there's a child grown up, the child is young again, half-wild, lost or drowning. The enemy might be a friend, the stranger your lover. Anyone can enter, any animal can come after you. Anything can come inside, only there is no inside, only darkness where you have been.

The Lost Hour

Maybe it's searching, calling to return, deciding who will disappear into it. And where does it go as it takes us into its clear arms?

The Light of Late Winter

> *I am an autumn child*
> —W.S. Merwin

It's deep in our bones, where we first sprouted
from the light. When I came into the world
just after spring arrived, there was that quiet
from long burial deeper than any snow cover
below where any root reaches
where there is no seed.

Passenger

The plane rattles through darkness and cold,
only she's sweating. When she opens her eyes,
she finds herself stranded, no longer
a passenger. Or is she alone in that plane with the roar
of its engine? Maybe her bed is the ground
made of what fell from the wings.

To the Darkness

Where did you begin
to live under the light
always there
a mystery inside the clear day
you hold us in your sleep and wakefulness
it is all the same
all the dreams of the sleeping & dying
voices & vowels, melodies & discords
all there though we can't see
or hear you guiding us like a hand in a dream
that doesn't let go but takes us through
wild terrains of the heart, its questions
& torments, hollows & swells
unknown beginnings & endings
all middle places where love once
opened & keeps opening, here all the thresholds
& pathways are blended, all the stains
& wounds absorbed, the scars & the scares
converged, the rocks all crushed
to black powder or liquid of grape into wine
grain of the sea into sea.

A Memory

I return to the memory of that first night.
It was winter. The light
opened parts of your face
I had never seen. You were someone
I had known a long time before
but never really known. Someone
who had long ago touched
and filled me with a dream
that doesn't die. In this dream
you are looking at me
with wonder, mystery and passion.
There is nothing after that.

To Sleep

I live with you
though not forever. Only you
can wash me, flowing through
and darkening whatever the day to night
to form memories that never happened,
but some of them make me weep
and others I recognize from another
unlived life. Sometimes I don't know
which world we belong to
without any borders or walls,
so clear is the dream.

Windy Night

Our house caught fire
when I was a child—
later I drew myself as a paper doll
penciling the eyes so
fervently I fell through
a burning floor where beams dissolved
into the unfathomable bed
of dreams that couldn't be stilled—
what flows through the world
like a single flame
lighting our eyes
when we open them.

Lost Book

This afternoon the pond appears radiant
with infinite sparks.
Heraclitus believed the soul was fire.
And so it burns
but is never consumed, its power
a secret that doesn't
stop flowing. Heraclitus's book
is lost in the light.

Paradoxical

The astronomer Olbers called
the universe a paradox
because its age is infinite with stars,
so the night should be made of light.
Joan of Arc cried out
as her body was eaten by flames,
but her heart was never consumed.
Maybe her voices carried her
into the oldest night
of this early spring dawn.

Flowers of Snow
> *The whole world all one cloud.*
> —Tu Fu

The way to grow invisible is to follow the path
of falling snow, to stand in the yard
on an April morning and hold out your hands
to take what falls onto your shoulders and the top
of your head, letting your face grow cold, your arms
and legs sink into the falling sky already on the budded
magnolia and just flowered peach trees, so when
you look up to millions of the ghostly falling
you might imagine, if you go out early and stand.

Birthday

This day holds an image of myself
young and alive by the window, waiting
for someone or something,
a bookmark in a book without words.
When I came into the world I didn't know
where or what we were.
When I was a child I made a boat in a garden.
I just remembered last night's dream
of watching a mother and baby rabbit
climb out of a pot, leaving
a brief wake in the wetness.

Ten Thousand Things

in that empty chair
in the statue of the fisherman
holding a rod with no line
in the guitar in its case
in the old dolls high on a shelf
staring straight ahead
in Billie Holliday's averted gaze.

After the Words

I live in the silent things, the stillness
of rooms after the light has left
and shadows have settled
the same inside as out.
What lies between the sleeping and the dead,
the flying and the feather that lies on the ground,
the memory and the future
because what we feel when we're dreaming
holds too much to see
as here in the words,
long after the words go silent.

Gazing at Branches
    for Kevin & Faye

The lower branches of the pine
are stunted, without needles.
They don't even look alive.
At the top each cluster opens to the sky.
As I write on a blank page
each word has another existence
that disappears into the whiteness.
Yesterday a hawk sat on one
of those broken branches.
I could barely make out its hunched form
till it spread its wings between us
awakening that endless place.

Open the Book to Any Page

and read the first word you see
It's *loom* today
The next *beneath*
and the third *enigma*
Color such great wild form
mutual falling sense material
that subject brightly reading
inheritance line energy weaves
star shape still
and mountains
come in become silent

Return

On the bog near dawn
a sandhill veiled
in fog. Emptiness surrounds
the mound words can't fill
with their brief scrawl
erased by the thought of
a chore, fragment of voice,
text ding, flash of news,
a reminder. Wanting
to return to this hill
I pass every day.

Without a Trace

Chekhov said nothing in this world is clear and believed the heart a wanderer, each of us making our way through one moment after another like phantoms, while the route we draw as we move is only remembered here and there, and though some of the detail is exquisite, it may never have existed, even as its lines are marked somewhere inside at the same time the heart is recording its every movement, though neither the heart nor its map can be unfolded, nor its wilderness be traced.

Amid Such Breath
> *Faye George (1934-2020) and Winston Bolton (1929-2020)*

Breath is everywhere today—
the needles of the fallen
pine branches look suddenly
alive as the dead leaves in spring
and fresh greens fill the hollows.
Even the woody hair of the grapevine
is blushed, while cries of the peepers
ring past the porch chimes
and a siren sings down the road,
the sound of your voices
still in my ear, but inside the chest
it is homeless. The chest grows tight,
while breath covers the roofs
like April sunshine. There aren't enough
body bags for all our breath.
Where do the breaths
of a body go? What clings
to the trees before they bloom?

Part of Me

This morning the darkness lies close
as the faint reflection of bookshelves
on the window. The words pressed
to their pages of whiteness. And the room
with its child rocker, empty shoes and lamplight
on the pillow leaning against the arm
of the blue sofa: these too come
from somewhere unknown, as a fresh spring
wind rushes from other parts of the world
where people lie sick and dying
during a pandemic no one can contain.
I can't see the wet branches
out my window, or feel where
the heart's blood comes from.

Barbara Siegel Carlson's third book *What Drifted Here* is due out from WordTech Communications in 2022. She is the author of two previous poetry collections *Once in Every Language* (Kelsay Books, 2017) and *Fire Road* (Dream Horse Press, 2013), co-translator of two books of poems by Srečko Kosovel *Open* (2018) and *Look Back, Look Ahead* (2010), and co-editor of *A Bridge of Voices: Contemporary Slovene Poetry and Perspectives* (2017). She is one of five poets featured in *Take Five*, a collection of prose poems (Finishing Line Press, 2020). Carlson is Poetry in Translation Editor of *Solstice*, teaches in Boston and lives in Carver, Massachusetts.

www.ingramcontent.com/pod-product-compliance
Lightning Source LLC
LaVergne TN
LVHW041521070426
835507LV00012B/1736